Bristol Libraries

Renewals 0845 002 0777
www.bristol.gov.uk/libraries

BI

21055 Print Servicess

D0229840

The History of
The Asian Community in Britain

Rozina Visram

An imprint of Hodder Children's Books

Titles in the History of Communities Series

The History of the African and Caribbean
  Communities in Britain

The History of the Asian Community
  in Britain

For my nephew, Farooq

First published in 1995 by Wayland Publishers Ltd

Copyright 1995 Hodder Wayland

Revised and updated in 2005 by Hodder Wayland,
an imprint of Hodder Children's Books

Series editor: Cath Senker
Book editor: Liz Harman
Designer: Jean Wheeler
Picture researcher: Liz Harman and Rozina Visram
Production controller: Carol Stevens
Cover design: Hodder Wayland

British Library Cataloguing in Publication Data

The History of the Asian Community in Britain. – (History
I. Title II. Series
941.00495

ISBN 0-7502-4736-3

Printed in China by WKT Company Ltd

Sources of quotes

1. *Sophie in London, 1786, being the Diary of Sophie v. la Roche* translated by C. Williams (Jonathan Cape, 1993)
2. *Lives of the Most Remarkable Criminals who had been condemned and executed for murder, highway robberies, house breaking . . . from 1720–1735* Volume I compiled from original sources and memoirs, 1874)
3. *London City Mission Magazine* (August 1922)
4. *London City Mission Magazine* (July 1900)
5. *Across Seven Seas and Thirteen Rivers: Life Stories of Pioneer Sylhetti Sailors in Britain* edited and compiled by Caroline Adams (THAP Books, 1987)
6. *London Labour and the London Poor* Volume III by H. Mayhew (Griffin, Bohn & Co, 1861)
7. *The New Scots: The Story of Asians in Scotland* by B. Maan (John Donald Publishers, 1992)
8. Caroline Adams, *Op. cit.*
9. *Ibid.*
10. *Them* by J. Green (Secker & Warburg, 1990)
11. *Destination Bradford* (Bradford Heritage Recording Unit, 1987)
12. J. Green, *Op. cit.*

Picture acknowledgements (t=top, b=bottom)
The authors and publishers would like to thank the following for allowing their pictures to be reproduced in this book: British Library 6, 11, 21 (t), 22, 23, 24 (b), 26 (b), 27; Camera Press 45 (t); Noel Channan 10; Communist Party Picture Library 25, Audrey Dewjee 38; East Sussex Libraries 19; Equal Opportunities Commission 44; Grange Museum, Neasden 44; HMSO 39; Hulton Deutsch 4, 5, 8 (t), 34, 41, 43; Imperial War Museum 26 (t), 36; London Borough of Enfield 8 (b); London Borough of Islington, Libraries Department 21 (b), 32, 33; Bashir Maan 30; Museum in Docklands, PLA Collection 12, 13, 21; Museum of London 14, 15 (t), 20, 24 (t), 24 (b); Museum of art, Sao Paulo, Brazil title page & 7; M. S. Pujji contents page & 37; Punch 15 (b); Queen Victoria Seamen's Rest 28; Royal Collection Enterprises 9, 17; The Royal Pavilion Art Gallery and Museums, Brighton 18; M. S. Simpson 29; Somerville College, Oxford 16; Tim Smith 40, 42, 45 (b); Rozina Visram 35. Cover image: www.johnbirdsall.co.uk

Contents

1

First settlers

As early as the 1630s, people from the Indian sub-continent, Asians, were living in Britain. Many of these early settlers were brought to Britain by the employees of the British East India Company, which was formed in 1600.

The East India Company wanted to cash in on the profitable spice trade of the East. But competition from the Dutch drove the company to India, which was ruled by a powerful Muslim dynasty, the Mughals. As a rich and sophisticated civilization, India was at the centre of a vast network of trade. From a few trading centres, called factories, the East India Company built up a profitable pattern of trade. This had a revolutionary effect on British economy and society.

An imperial procession in India in 1813.

From trade to Empire

During its early years in India the East India Company did not interfere in Indian politics. However, in the eighteenth century, it became more powerful. The company had its own army, which it used to conquer territories. In 1757 Bengal, one of the wealthiest provinces of the Mughal empire, was conquered. Then, as the Mughal empire declined, the company, using its military superiority, gradually extended British rule over a large part of India. The British Empire in India lasted until 1947.

British control of India, through trade, conquest and colonization, resulted in a gradual migration of many classes of Asians to Britain. Some, like servants and sailors, were brought by their employers. Others, like students, chose to come. Indian soldiers fought in British wars. In India, political and economic changes introduced by the British drove others to look for work in Britain. Politicians came to fight for justice and freedom. Others came to trade and establish businesses. Some, like princes, were rich but the majority of Asians who came to Britain were poor. British reaction to the settlers varied; some were accepted but others faced hostility and prejudice.

This photograph, taken in India in 1881, shows the Indian and European staff of the Executive Engineers' Office. Indian employees of British people working in India often returned with them to Britain and made their home there.

Servants

The earliest Asian settlers came to Britain as servants of the employees of the East India Company. From its very beginning in 1600, employment with the company was very popular among young British men. They went to India as clerks, traders and soldiers hoping to make their fortune. Many did, creating a new class of rich men, the 'nabobs', who returned to Britain to live like the aristocracy. The nabobs bought seats in Parliament and estates in the country. They brought their Indian servants with them and tried to recreate the luxurious lifestyle they had enjoyed in India.

Sezincote in Gloucestershire, home of the nabob Charles Cockerell, whose fortune was made in India.

Notice the Indian architecture, copied from the Taj Mahal.

In the seventeenth and eighteenth centuries many rich families in Britain had Asian (and African) servants. This was considered very fashionable. Asian servants were thought to be exotic and were often treated like pets. A German visitor to Daylesford House, Worcestershire in 1786 described the Indian servants of Warren Hastings:

'The two Indian boys, thirteen or fourteen years old ... have longish faces, beautiful eyes, fine eyebrows, sleek black hair, thin lips, fine teeth, a brownish complexion and kingly, intelligent faces.'[1]

Servants' lives

Finding out about the lives of Asian servants in Britain is difficult. Their duties were similar to those of other domestic servants, but evidence suggests that their lives were often lonely and difficult. Asian servants could be dismissed, given away or even sold by their employers.

This is the story of a seventeen-year-old boy called Julian:

> 'He had been stolen while young from his parents at Madras. He still retained his Pagan Ignorance in respect to Religion and our Language. He was brought over by Captain Dawes, who presented him to Mrs Elizabeth Turner, where he was used with the greatest Tenderness and Kindness, often calling him in to dance and sing after his Manner before Company ... Yet on a Sudden, he stole about twenty or thirty Guineas, and then placing a Candle under the Sheets, left it burning to fire the House ... He ended his Life at Tyburn [prison] according to his Sentence.'[2]

The children of Edward Holden Cruttenden with an 'ayah' (nanny), painted by Joshua Reynolds in 1759.

7

Two British men with their Indian servants stop by a roadside in Buji State, India, for 'tiffin' (a light meal).

Some Asian servants ran away, sometimes taking their owners' property with them. Employers whose servants had run away placed 'hue and cry' notices in the newspapers, describing the servants and asking for help in finding them.

In the nineteenth century, as British industries expanded, there was a demand for more raw materials like tea, jute and rubber. Large plantations were established in India to grow these crops. Planter families living in Britain sometimes employed Asian servants in their homes.

The fashion for Indian servants did not end in the eighteenth century. Sundhi Din, a Glasgow hawker in the 1920s and '30s, for instance, came to Britain as a valet to a Scottish army officer some time before the First World War.

In this picture, dated about 1900, Thomas Lipton and his guests are served tea by his Asian servants in the tree house in the grounds of his house in north London. Lipton owned many tea plantations in Ceylon (now Sri Lanka).

Abdul Karim, Queen Victoria's munshi, *painted by Rudolf Swoboda in 1888.*

Servants to royalty

Queen Victoria became Empress of India in 1877, but she never went there. In 1887, after her Golden Jubilee, several Indian servants and their wives joined the royal household. Abdul Karim, the *munshi* (teacher), was the queen's favourite. He later became her secretary. The queen took lessons in Hindustani from him and encouraged ladies at court to do the same. Abdul Karim received the title of 'Companion of the Indian Empire', a great honour. All this attention given to an Indian servant horrified the court and, after Queen Victoria's death, Abdul Karim was sent back to India.

Queen Victoria's son, Edward VII, began the custom of appointing Indian Orderly Officers as his special bodyguard. After 1903, four Indian Officers attended the king every year during the London season between April and August.

Ayahs

From the period of the East India Company to the end of British rule in 1947, travel to India was by ship. British families employed Asian nannies, called ayahs, to look after their children during the long voyage back to Britain. The families were expected to provide return passages for the ayahs, but many did not. Once in England, the nannies were discharged and left to make their own way home. Some were able to get a passage back to India by advertising in newspapers for positions as servants to British people travelling to India. But some ayahs were permanently stranded in Britain and their plight was recorded in this letter in the Public Advertiser in December 1786:

This is a 'carte' (calling card). It shows Alexandra, Princess of Wales, with her baby, Louise, and an Indian ayah.

'Sir

When a family returns from India, they generally bring over with them one or more female blacks to take care of the children, under promise to send them back to their native country free of expense ... the number of those poor wretches who are daily begging for a passage back, proves that ... those who bring them over leave them to shift for [look after] themselves the moment they have no further occasion for their services. Many of them, I am informed, have been in England two or three years; and some of them must forever remain here.'

The Ayahs' Home was opened in London in 1897. Every year two or three hundred nannies from India (and China) stayed there. Families travelling to India came to the Home to engage nannies.

Mrs Antony Pareira was a travelling Indian ayah. She was a widow who was:

> ... very brown and wrinkled ... smiling and complacent, gentle and maternal, soft-spoken and plainly self-reliant, with small dark eyes alight with keen intelligence. No fewer than fifty-four times had this nurse of the turbulent ocean made the journey between India and Great Britain and once to Holland ... Herself a mother at sixteen, she had been these many years possessed of grandsons and granddaughters.'[3]

A photograph of a group of ayahs spending their time in various activities at the Ayahs' Home in Hackney, London in 1900.

Lascars

Other Asians came to Britain as sailors on British ships bringing cargo from the East. Before the days of steamships, the voyage to India took nearly a year. Illness was common among the British crew. Some died and others deserted in India. To make up the numbers on the return trip, the East India Company employed Indian sailors, called 'lascars', to serve on their ships. The ships were called East Indiamen. Lascars were not permanent settlers in Britain. They stayed in port until their ship was ready to sail again. As trade expanded, more ships arrived and the number of lascars increased. Shipping companies often preferred to employ lascars because they were paid less than European sailors. When steamships replaced East Indiamen, lascars worked as firemen, stoking the ships' furnaces with coal. Sometimes the entire crew was Asian, as this account tells us:

This photograph, which was taken in 1908, shows Asian sailors, known as lascars, on board a ship at the East India Dock, London.

'... one Company whose steamers carry emigrants to Brisbane and return with cargoes of frozen meat have installed lascars on nearly all their ships instead of English sailors. The Royal Albert Docks is never without the presence of a large number of natives, frequently one thousand at a time.'[4]

European sailors did not like to work as firemen. This account, by a Bengali fireman, explains why:

> 'I was called a bunkerman, in the coal bunker ... It is a most difficult job, very hard and very hot too. Many people died in that heat. In my sea life, I knew hundreds of people who died.'[5]

Poverty drove Asian peasants to work as sailors, suffering ill-treatment, sickness and long waits in British ports. Pay and conditions were very poor. Born in British-ruled India, the lascars were considered British, but shipping companies employed them on contracts known as 'Asiatic Articles'. Under this system they were paid less than all other sailors. The 1910 Parliamentary Report tells us that Asian sailors received eight or nine shillings a week but, as the cost of a month's lodging was

Seamen waiting to see the doctor at the Well Street Seamen's Hospital, London, in 1881.

about forty-eight shillings, it is not surprising that some sailors deserted their ships. Deserters hoped to continue seafaring from Britain but on 'European Articles', which could double or even treble their wages. In time, small settlements of Asian sailors grew up in ports like Cardiff, Glasgow, Liverpool and London.

2
Earning a living

An Asian with his son, selling Christian tracts on the streets of Victorian London.

By the nineteenth century, a diverse group of Asians lived in Britain. Some were professionals, other were rich. The majority were poor and found it hard to make a living. Working-class Asians who were able to get a job usually worked as servants or sailors. Servants often advertised in newspapers for jobs as domestics. Obtaining work was difficult as there was strong competition. Prejudice was never far away, as this report in the *Glasgow Herald* of 21 April 1914 shows:

Asiatic Seamen
Transport workers' protest

A demonstration in furtherance of the agitation against the employment of Asiatic seamen on British ships was held last night in the City Hall at Glasgow ...

Their objection to Chinese and Indian labour was not because these men were of a different race and different colour, but because they lowered the standard of life for white men ...

Asians who were unable to find permanent jobs had to rely on their wits to survive. In the 1880s, a man called Grannee Manoo earned a living by selling old shoes that he had obtained by begging. One lascar sold half-penny ballads (song sheets) and his takings amounted to fifteen shillings a day, enabling him to live well. But many Asians simply scraped a living as hawkers or entertainers. Ram Sam, a well-known character, played a drum around London for fifteen years. Some Asians swept street crossings for pennies. Sailors, unable to get seafaring jobs, set up lodging houses, in places like Cardiff, Liverpool, Glasgow, London and Birmingham.

This is the story of a Calcutta-born Asian who had come to Britain as the servant of an army officer. After his master died, he worked for other families. Later, he moved to London. He married an English woman, and had a son. In 1861, when he had been living in Britain for ten years, he said.

'It is near five year I come to London. I try get service, but not get service. I have character [reference] ... I put up many insult in dis countree. I struck sometime in street ... Wen I get no service ... I not beg ... I buy tom-tom for 10 shillings ... my last money left, and I start to play in streets for daily bread. I beat tom-tom, and sing song about greatness of God, in my own language ... I done pretty well first ... I make three shillings, four shillings, five shillings, six shillings a day ... but nine or ten monts it was something old, and I took less and less, until now I hardly get a piece of bread. I sometime get a few shillings from two or three picture-men who draw me. It is call model. Anything for honest bread. I must not be proud.'[6]

The street herbalist, Doctor Bokanky, selling medicines in Victorian London.

This cartoon from the magazine Punch, *in 1848, shows an unkind view of an Asian crossing sweeper.*

Professionals

A few Asians were more successful. They were traders and merchants. In 1858, the firm of Cama and Company became the first Asian merchant house to open in London and there was also a branch in Liverpool.

Middle-class Asians living in Britain worked in a variety of professions. For example, George Edalji was a solicitor in Birmingham and his father, Shapurji Edalji, was appointed vicar in Great Wyrley, Staffordshire, in 1876. Other Asians taught at British universities and many others had come to study. One of these was Cornelia Sorabji, the first-ever woman law student at a British university. She studied at Oxford from 1889 to 1894. Some Asian students trained to be doctors, like Pulipaka Jagannadham, who qualified in Edinburgh and established a practice there in 1892.

Cornelia Sorabji was the first woman in Britain to study law. But, even after qualifying, she could not work as a lawyer because women were barred from the legal profession until 1919.

Wealthy Asians, like Prince Ranjitsinhji, also came to Britain to study. Ranji was an undergraduate at Cambridge from 1889 to 1893. He seized the public's imagination because he played cricket for Sussex from 1895 and was the captain for five years. He was also the first Asian cricketer to play for England. Another member of the Asian nobility was Maharajah Duleep Singh. When the British took over the Punjab in 1849, he was exiled to Britain, where he lived the life of a country squire at Elveden in Norfolk.

Maharajah Duleep Singh, aged about sixteen, painted by F. X. Winterhalter in 1854. This portrait was specially painted for Queen Victoria.

Sake Deen Mahomed

The most well-known professional Asian in nineteenth-century England was Sake Deen Mahomed. He was born in Patna, India, in 1759. When he was ten he joined Captain Baker, an officer in the East India Regiment. His book, *Travels of Dean Mahomet*, was published in Ireland in 1794. It describes the conquest of India by the East India Company from an Indian point of view. In 1784 Mahomed came to Britain with Captain Baker. They settled in Cork, Ireland, where Mahomed met his future wife, Jane, with whom he eloped to get married.

Sake Deen Mohamed, whose reputation for curing illness was considered by some people to be a reason for the growth of Brighton.

From Cork, Mahomed moved to London, where he ran a coffee house. Later he went to Brighton, a popular health resort. In those days people believed that bathing in sea water cured rheumatism. There were many indoor baths in Brighton. Mahomed opened his Vapour Baths and Shampooing (massaging) Establishment in 1815. His treatment was new: patients first soaked themselves in a steaming bath of Indian herbs and oils, then they were given a massage. Mahomed believed that this was a powerful cure for rheumatic illnesses.

However, Mahomed met with prejudice and medical opposition, and patients stayed away. Not discouraged, he offered free treatment to some patients and they found that his remedies worked where others had failed. This was the beginning of Mahomed's success. As his fame spread, fashionable people from all over Britain and Europe flocked to Mahomed's baths, and doctors sent their patients to him. King George IV appointed Mahomed as his personal 'Shampooing Surgeon' in 1822, an appointment which William IV continued. Mahomed was a generous man and even treated the poor free of charge.

In 1822, Mahomed's medical book, *Shampooing or Benefits Resulting from the Use of Indian Medical Vapour Bath*, was published, and was very popular. His success influenced others to set up shampooing baths in Brighton. A rival establishment, Molineaux's, opened in 1825 while, in 1868, the Turkish Bath Company opened the Turkish Hamam.

Mahomed died in 1851. His son, Horatio, opened a shampooing establishment at St James's in London. Another son, Frederick, ran a fencing academy in Brighton with his wife. One grandson, James Kerriman Mahomed (1853–1935), was a vicar in Hove. Another grandson, Frederick Akbar Mahomed (1849–1884), a doctor at Guy's Hospital in London, was a pioneer of 'collective investigation'. This is a system of collecting information on diseases from questionnaires sent to doctors throughout the country, and it is still in use today.

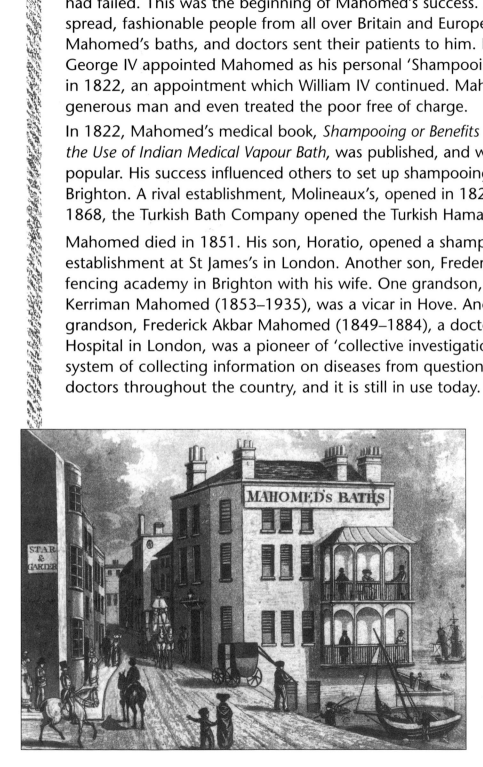

Mohamed's Baths on the sea front in Brighton.

3
Political voices

After an election in Deptford, south London in 1886, the losing candidate, a popular Asian politician named Mr Lalmohun Ghose, was cheered. The winner was booed.

In India, people saw many changes to their lives under colonialism. There were revolts against the British and, after a large but unsuccessful uprising in 1857, resistance took different forms. Many Indians challenged the view that British rule brought benefits to India. In the unequal colonial relationship Indians lost out. Their industries, such as textiles, were destroyed as cheap British cotton flooded the market. Areas of India that were once wealthy were reduced to poverty. In order to pay their taxes, Indian farmers were forced to grow crops like jute, needed for British industries, rather than food for the people. Indian people paid taxes but had no say in the government of their country, which was controlled by the British. Most jobs in the civil service were held by white people. Even the exam to enter the service was held in Britain, and most Indians could not afford to travel to Britain to take it.

Taking action

Associations were formed to campaign for justice and independence from the British. The Indian National Congress, founded in 1884, was the most influential. Some British people supported the Indians and, in Britain, societies were formed to help Indian nationalists. One of these was the British Committee of the Indian National Congress, whose members spoke up for Indian independence in Parliament.

Some Indian nationalists brought the campaign to Britain, hoping to educate people about British rule in India. Some of them tried to stand for Parliament. Since all laws concerning India were made in the British Parliament, it made sense to have Indian representatives there. But in the late nineteenth century, when Asians tried to get into Parliament, they found that, although they were British citizens, it was no easy matter.

This Indian cartoon, from 1892, shows India weighed down by military expenditure and taxes. Asians believed that India 'bore the burden' of the British Empire.

Dadabhai Naoroji

Dadabhai Naoroji was a mathematician and economist. In 1855 he came to London as a partner in the Asian merchant firm, Cama and Company. Naoroji quickly became a respected voice for India by writing letters to newspapers and speaking at meetings. In 1878 Naoroji wrote a book called *Poverty of India*. In this book, he said that Britain 'drained' India of £30–40 million every year, causing poverty and hardship but making British industrialists rich. Many MPs consulted him about the effects of British rule in India.

CASE
study

An 1895 election poster, showing Dadabhai Naoroji.

Naoroji joined the Liberal Party and stood for Parliament. At his second attempt, in 1892, he succeeded in becoming the first Asian MP by winning a seat in Finsbury, north London, by a narrow majority of just five votes. Naoroji was considered a model MP. He supported important issues like free education, public housing and self-governing powers for London, Home Rule for Ireland, and votes for women.

Naoroji also spoke out in Parliament in favour of justice for India. He began as a moderate nationalist, believing in British justice and fair play. Naoroji campaigned to achieve representation for Indians in the government of India. But he was disappointed by his lack of success, and became a strong campaigner for *swaraj* (self-rule).

Naoroji was an MP for only three years. When, in 1895, the Liberal Party was swept from power, Naoroji lost his seat. In 1900 he stood again as a Liberal in Lambeth, south London but was unsuccessful.

The Indian Home Rule Society

In 1905 a radical student organization called the Indian Home Rule Society was established. The society was prepared to use violence to get rid of British rule in India. The students met at India House in Highgate, north London, where they discussed plans to free India. Members took lessons in revolver shooting. The British government planted informers from Scotland Yard to spy on their activities. The student agitation reached a climax in July 1909 when a member of the society, Madan Lal Dhingra, assassinated the Political Aide-de-Camp Sir William Curzon Wyllie. Dhingra was hanged in Pentonville Prison in August 1909.

Madan Lal Dhingra, who said that he was glad 'to have the honour of dying for [my] country.'

Sir Mancherjee Bhownaggree

The second Asian to be elected for Parliament was a Conservative. Sir Mancherjee Bhownaggree was a lawyer from a wealthy family, who had settled in London in 1891. He became MP for Bethnal Green, in the East End of London, in 1895, and worked hard to improve conditions for the people living there. Bhownaggree was so popular that he was elected again in 1900, but lost his seat in 1906 when the Conservatives were defeated by the Liberals. Unlike Naoroji, Bhownaggree was not critical of British rule in India, believing that it helped India. He was popular with the Conservative Party in Britain, but not in India.

CASE
study

A cartoon from the Indian press, dated 1896, illustrating Indian opinion at Bhownaggree's election triumph as a Conservative.

The role of women

Asian women also took part in politics. In 1911, members of the Women's Social and Political Union organized a Women's Coronation Procession to publicize their campaign for the vote. The procession stretched eleven kilometres, and many suffragette organizations took part, including Indian suffragettes. Little is known about Asian suffragettes. Sophia Duleep Singh, who lived in London, was an active campaigner for votes for women.

◀ *Sophia Duleep Singh selling the suffragette newspaper outside Hampton Court Palace in 1913.*

▼ *Asian women marching for the vote in the procession organized by the suffragettes in London in 1911.*

Shapurji Saklatvala

It was not until 1922 that another Asian became an MP. Shapurji Saklatvala was the nephew of pioneering Bombay industrialist J.N. Tata, but despite his wealthy background, Saklatvala became a champion of the working class. In 1905 he came to Britain for medical treatment. Saklatvala became active in working-class politics and joined the Workers Union and the Independent Labour Party. After the Communist Party was founded in 1920, he became a member. In 1922 he was elected MP for the constituency of Battersea, in South London.

CASE study

Saklatvala addressing a meeting in Trafalgar Square, London in June 1922.

Saklatvala was a powerful speaker, a great advantage in the days of large public gatherings. He spoke on behalf of the working classes in Britain who were suffering from mass unemployment, poverty and poor housing. Saklatvala believed that capitalism exploited the workers in Britain just as colonialism exploited the workers in India. He never tired of campaigning for the workers of both countries and spoke up for the rights of Asians in Britain.

During the General Strike of 1926, Saklatvala was arrested and charged with sedition for a speech he made in Hyde Park, urging the soldiers not to fire on striking workers. He was imprisoned for two months.

Saklatvala lost his parliamentary seat in 1923, but regained it in 1924, with a large majority. He remained Battersea's MP until 1929, and in 1930 he unsuccessfully contested a by-election in Glasgow.

4

The First World War

Going into battle

During the First World War, India provided Britain with 1.3 million soldiers. Of these, 138,000 Indian troops fought on the Western Front, at Ypres in Belgium, and at Neuve Chapelle and Loos in France. They arrived just in time, since the British Expeditionary Force had been almost wiped out. Indians also fought in Gallipoli, Mesopotamia, the Middle East and East Africa. Thousands of Indian sailors were recruited by the Merchant Navy and as many as 3,427 lost their lives. Many Indian soldiers received medals, but thousands had died and thousands more were maimed for life.

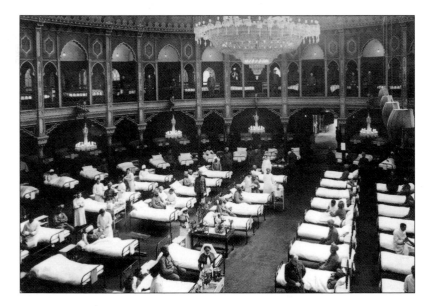

◄ *Wounded Indian soldiers in the Pavilion and Dome Hospital, Brighton.*

▼ *Indian soldiers in a trench on the Western Front in October 1914.*

The aftermath

When the First World War ended, many Asian sailors discharged in Britain were stranded, as jobs on ships were scarce. Times were hard for everyone and Britain went through a period of poverty and unemployment. Despite their efforts in the war, Asians were no longer welcome in Britain. This was demonstrated by this report in *The Times* of 30 May 1919:

'Large crowds assembled outside the Asiatic Home in West India Dock Road and any coloured man who appeared was greeted with abuse and had to be escorted by the police. It was necessary at times to bar the doors of the Home.'

THIS STONE
WAS ERECTED BY
PARISHIONERS OF BROCKENHURST,
TO MARK THE SPOT WHERE IS LAID
THE EARTHLY BODY OF
SUKHA,
A RESIDENT OF MOHULLA, GUNGAPUR,
CITY BARIELLY, UNITED PROVINCES OF INDIA.
HE LEFT COUNTRY, HOME & FRIENDS, TO SERVE OUR
KING & EMPIRE, IN THE GREAT EUROPEAN WAR.
AS A HUMBLE SERVANT IN THE LADY HARDINGE
HOSPITAL FOR WOUNDED INDIAN SOLDIERS
IN THIS PARISH,
HE DEPARTED THIS LIFE ON JANUARY 12TH 1915,
AGED 30 YEARS.
BY CREED, HE WAS NOT "CHRISTIAN",
BUT HIS EARTHLY LIFE WAS SACRIFICED IN THE
INTERESTS OF OTHERS.
"THERE IS ONE GOD AND FATHER OF ALL; WHO IS
OVER ALL, AND THROUGH ALL, AND IN ALL."
EPHESIANS. IV. 6.

In 1920, the Labour Exchange sent four lascars, who had served in the war, to work at the Kingshill Colliery in Lanarkshire, Scotland. Other Asians worked in the iron and steel works around Lanarkshire. There was an outcry at the employment of this 'cheap' labour. Questions were asked in Parliament and there were calls for their repatriation. In 1925 the Glasgow Indian Union wrote to the government protesting about the treatment of its members. The Asians were British citizens because they had been born in India. But the police were trying to use the 1925 Coloured Alien Seamen's Order to force them to return to India, even though many had been in Britain for over fourteen years. Protest and prejudice forced some Asians, like the stranded lascars, into self-employment, becoming hawkers and pedlars.

Many civilians were also recruited from Indian to help the war effort. They came to look after wounded Indian soldiers. This is a photograph of the gravestone of one of these civilians, Sukha.

Kamal Chunchie

Long after the war, life for Black seamen in Britain remained harsh. It was among this community that Kamal Chunchie worked. Chunchie was a police inspector from Ceylon (now Sri Lanka). When war broke out in 1914, he enlisted in the Public Schools Battalion in Ceylon. He was one of the few Black soldiers in the British army and the only one in his battalion to fight in Europe.

Chunchie became a Christian and, in 1922, he joined the Methodist Mission. His area of work was London's docklands, where the condition of African and Asian seamen shocked Chunchie. Like himself, many of them were married to White women and were the victims of hostility and racism. Lack of work, both at sea and on shore, had reduced them to wretched poverty.

The staff of Queen Victoria Seamen's Mission in 1922. Kamal Chunchie is third from the left in the back row.

In 1926 Chunchie began a new branch of the Mission, called the Coloured Men's Institute, in Canning Town, east London. It became a religious, welfare and recreational centre for the Black community. Chunchie preached to large audiences, visited the sick and ran a Sunday school. With money raised by donations and subscriptions, he organized outings to the seaside and gave clothing, shoes, coal and food to those in need. Chunchie was a keen sportsman and, despite his busy life, even found time to play cricket for Essex.

In 1930 the Coloured Men's Institute was demolished when the road was widened. Chunchie campaigned to raise money for a new building, but funds were short and his house in Lewisham, south London, became his base. All through the Second World War and beyond, Chunchie continued working in the docklands. He died in 1953.

A mixed group of Londoners at a New Year children's party held at the Victoria Dock Road Presbyterian Church in 1937. Kamal Chunchie organized parties every year for the Black community.

5

The Asian community in the 1930s

The Asian community in Britain increased gradually during the 1920s and '30s because economic opportunities in India were limited. Indian industries were not developed, so the majority of people earned a living by farming. Since plots were small, farmers fell into debt. Young men were driven to look for employment as sailors and soldiers, in India, or elsewhere in the Empire. Some adventurous young men came to Britain and stayed for a few years, sometimes returning for another spell of work.

Pedlars

Asian pedlars often lived in groups and helped each other. Kartar Singh Seran, who came to Britain in 1932, remembers that their homes:

> '... were dilapidated properties, in a state of utter disrepair ... We had a common kitchen; food was cooked in turn by one member of the group for all. A newcomer was fed and clothed and looked after ... until he was able to stand on his own feet.'[7]

Nathoo Mohammed

CASE study

Nathoo Mohammed is typical of the settlers of the 1930s. He had been a farmer in India, and then worked as a stoker on a ship. In about 1921 Mohammed bought a passenger ticket and came to Glasgow. Britain was suffering a depression and work was scarce, so he became a pedlar. With a vendor's licence and a suitcase full of clothes, Mohammed set out on his weekly rounds. Later, he married a Scottish woman and set up his own fabric shop in Glasgow.

Nathoo Mohammed, from the Punjab, earned his living as a pedlar in Scotland in the 1920s.

Pedlars worked in places as different as Chatham in Kent, Lewis in the Outer Hebrides, Cardiff and Manchester. In areas where shops were scarce, pedlars provided a useful service, bringing consumer goods to the doorstep. If they were able to save enough money, some pedlars opened drapery stores.

K. Rewachand had an artificial silk and hosiery business in Poplar, London, and employed agents in Britain and Ireland. He had customers in places as far apart as Inverness, Norwich and Torquay.

Sailors

In 1938 an East London newspaper reported an increase in Stepney's Asian population. Many of these newcomers were lascars who had jumped ship because of poverty. Men like Surat Alley, a trade unionist, campaigned for higher wages for Asian sailors but pay remained low. Many lascars took jobs as 'errand boys' for tailors. Londoners considered these jobs unsuitable because they had poor prospects and pay. But, as errand boys, Asians earned more than they could as sailors.

Asian sailors unloading cargo on the Royal Albert Dock, London, in 1930.

Chunilal Katial

CASE study

Chunilal Katial became the first Asian mayor in Britain in 1938. Already a qualified doctor, he came to Britain in 1927 for further training. His first practice was in the East End of London where, in 1931, he welcomed Mahatma Gandhi during his visit to Britain. In 1933 Katial moved to Finsbury, north London. His surgery was so popular that it was said that 'the difference between East and West did not exist there.' Before the National Health Service (NHS) doctors also had to run a private practice in order to make enough money. Katial had a private practice in Harley Street.

The winning Labour team on Finsbury Council after the elections in 1934. Dr Katial is in the front row, third from the left.

In 1934 Katial was elected as a Labour councillor in Finsbury. Housing in Finsbury was poor and there was overcrowding, ill-health and disease. Before the NHS was started, health facilities were haphazard. As chairman of the Public Health Committee, Katial fought for a new health centre which would provide up-to-date facilities under one roof. There was some opposition but Katial's hopes were realized with the opening of the Finsbury Health Centre in 1938.

During the Second World War Katial joined the civil defence force, and was a first-aid medical officer. In 1948 Katial was awarded the Freedom of the Borough of Finsbury, for his services to the people of the area.

A 1938 photograph of Finsbury Health Centre in Pine Street, Islington, London.

Government hostility

We do not really know how big the Asian community was in the 1930s. At the most it numbered a few thousand people, both rich and poor, scattered around Britain in cities and towns. The growth of the working-class Asian population in Britain created anxiety. From about 1931, the British government began to look for ways to stop Asian immigration. It wanted to discourage lascars from deserting their ships and settling in Britain. It was also worried about the number of poor Asians who lived as pedlars. The government wanted to stop poor, uneducated Asians from coming to Britain, so it made it difficult for them to obtain a passport for travel to Britain.

Jainti Saggar

Saggar Street in Dundee is named after the Saggar family, who were doctors. The founder of the medical practice was Jainti Saggar. In 1919 Saggar came to Scotland to study medicine. He opened his surgery in 1925 and soon had a thriving practice. Saggar joined the Labour Party and, in 1936, was elected as a councillor, serving on Dundee Council for the next eighteen years. Saggar's areas of responsibility were education and health. Saggar was active in the Labour and Trade Union movements, and became secretary of the Dundee Town Council Labour Group. The Saggar medical practice continues today.

CASE study

Mahatma Gandhi turned the Indian National Congress into a mass movement. This picture shows Gandhi at an East End estate in 1931, during his visit to London for talks with the British government.

Campaigning for rights

In the late nineteenth century, Asians like Naoroji had campaigned in Britain for Indian independence. They had tried to obtain the support of White British people, but with limited success. After the First World War, Indian activists in Britain were more successful in their campaign for public support.

In 1919, unarmed Indian civilians were massacred at a peaceful gathering at Amritsar in India. The Indians now realized that the British were determined to rule India by force, and that they did not mean to fulfil their promises of self-government for India. Gandhi called for non-cooperation with the government and Indians stepped up demands for *swaraj*. Under Gandhi's leadership, civil disobedience campaigns began, but were brutally put down by the British government.

Krishna Menon

A man who was in the forefront of the struggle for independence was Krishna Menon. Born in Calicut, south India, Menon taught history for five years before coming to Britain in 1924 to study for a teaching diploma. Here, he founded a nationalist organization called the India League and began to campaign for Indian independence.

Krishna Menon campaigned to educate British people about the situation in India. He addressed meetings all over the country, speaking to students, miners, factory workers, women's groups and church organizations. He organized rallies, wrote to newspapers and published pamphlets. The Indian League became a large movement with branches all over Britain. Most of its supporters were White people, but Indians in Britain were also members. Volunteers worked tirelessly against government propaganda. Contacts were established inside Parliament, especially among Labour MPs. In 1932 Menon accompanied three Labour MPs on a fact-finding trip to India. Their report, *Condition of India*, gave a shocking picture of repression under British rule.

In this house from 1924 to 1947 lived V. K. KRISHNA MENON St. Pancras Borough Councillor 1934-1947 Honorary Freeman 1955 High Commissioner for India 1947-1952

In 1934 Menon was elected as a Labour councillor for St Pancras, London. For the next fourteen years he worked on behalf of the slum dwellers of St Pancras and continued his campaign for the people of India. In Camden, Menon was very effective as Chairman of the Library Committee, opening branch libraries and establishing a mobile service. He set up a book week and children's library, and organized arts and cultural events for the benefit of the people. During the Second World War St Pancras was badly bombed. Menon joined the civil defence and was an air-raid warden.

This plaque, outside Krishna Menon's old home at 57 Camden Square, was put up by Camden Council in 1974.

Despite all these activities, Menon found time to study, edit books for publishers and work as a solicitor. He was a man of vision, whose work in the India League helped to sway public opinion in Britain and prepare the way for India's freedom. Menon died in 1974.

6

The Second World War

When the Second World War began in 1939, the British Viceroy, who governed India, declared war without consulting the Indian National Congress leaders. India joined the battle to defeat Germany.

Joining the forces

Asians living in Britain were called up for service and helped the war effort in various ways. They played their part as doctors, engineers and workers in factories and fought in the army, navy and air force. Two and a half million soldiers of the Indian army fought overseas, mainly against Japan in Malaya (now Malaysia) and Burma. They also fought in the Middle East and North Africa, as well as in France and Italy. At Dunkirk, in France, 300 Indians were taken prisoner. The rest were evacuated and stationed in Britain. Many lost their lives at Monte Cassino in the final battle against the Italians.

An Asian family sheltering in the crypt of Christ Church in Spitalfields, east London, during the Blitz, November 1940.

OCTOBER 1940

Portrait by
Miss. PEARL FREEMAN
9 BERKELEY STREET
PICCADILLY. W.

Squadron Leader Mahendra Pujji, who joined the RAF in 1940, was born in Simla, Calcutta in India in 1918. He qualified as a pilot in 1937.

Squadron Leader Mahendra Pujji

Pilots from India came to Britain to volunteer for the Royal Air Force (RAF). Squadron Leader Mahendra Pujji was among the first twenty-four to volunteer, and describes how the pilots were given 'lord-like' treatment. He remembers the Battle of Britain and, of his time in the RAF, he says:

'I carried out sweeps over the enemy-occupied territory, escorted heavy bombers and was involved in many dog fights with German fighter planes ... Once when I was over France, my aircraft received a direct hit and my engine caught fire. I was lucky and just managed to reach the English coast. Though my aircraft was a total wreck, I escaped with minor injuries.'[8]

Asian sailors

As in the First World War, Asians in the Merchant Navy made an important contribution to the war effort. The Merchant Navy, with its 59,000 Asian sailors, played a vital role in the Second World War, keeping supply lines open. The sailors brought food and raw materials to Britain, braving many dangers like mines and torpedoes. This is how one Bengali sailor described his narrow escape in the waters of the Baltic:

> 'I jumped into the water ... very cold ... I was in the water, swimming around and holding on to a piece of wood for twelve hours before somebody came and picked us up.'[9]

Thousands of Asian sailors died. A Monument at Tower Hill in London records the names of only a few. The majority remain nameless.

The war effort in India

Asian veterans of the two world wars at their first annual reunion in Southall, London, in 1986.

War needs a large reservoir of people. Armies need weapons and machinery, uniforms and boots. India provided vital resources, but more were needed.

Indian factories could not increase production because they did not have the skilled workers, so Indians, known as Bevin Boys, were sent to train in Britain. The first batch of fifty arrived in 1941 and others followed. They were placed in factories throughout Britain. On their return to India, their new skills helped to increase India's output.

Noor Inayat Khan

Noor Inayat Khan was born in Moscow in 1914 and grew up in London. In 1920, her family settled in Paris.

In 1940 France fell to Hitler. Noor trained as a nurse with the French Red Cross. When the family was evacuated to England, she joined the Women's Auxiliary Air Force and trained as a wireless operator.

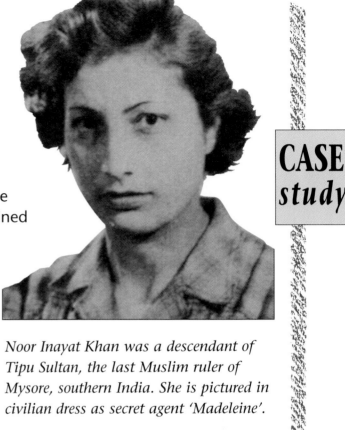

Noor Inayat Khan was a descendant of Tipu Sultan, the last Muslim ruler of Mysore, southern India. She is pictured in civilian dress as secret agent 'Madeleine'.

CASE *study*

Then Noor was invited to the War Office. She was told that secret agents were urgently needed in France. She knew Paris and spoke French fluently. Would she be willing to work for the French Resistance? Noor promptly volunteered. After a hasty training, she was flown out behind the lines in June 1943 and was given the code name 'Madeleine'. Noor became the first woman wireless operator in occupied France. Her task was to sabotage the German war machine, a dangerous mission.

Shortly after Noor arrived in Paris, the network was raided by the Gestapo and many agents were arrested. Noor chose to stay at her post and was one of only two wireless operators working in Paris. For three and a half months she remained a vital link between the War Office in London and the Paris resistance. Eventually she was betrayed. She returned to her flat one evening to find the Gestapo waiting for her. She was arrested and taken to Gestapo Headquarters. They transferred her to a prison in Germany where she remained for ten months. Then on 6 July 1944, with three other women agents, Noor Inayat Khan was taken to Dachau concentration camp and shot.

She was posthumously awarded the *Croix de Guerre* in 1946 and the George Cross in 1949.

7

Making a new life

During the time of British rule in India, many classes of Asians came to Britain. After the Second World War, some Asians who had served in the war decided to remain in Britain. A new pattern in Asian migration began between the 1950s and '70s, when a combination of economic and political developments led thousands of Asians from the Indian sub-continent and East Africa to make a new life in Britain.

Push and pull

Why did Asians decide to come to live and work in Britain? Historians sometimes describe the reasons as 'push and pull'. After the war the economy in Britain had to be rebuilt. This was a time of great social change. The NHS was set up, slums were cleared and new houses built, and industries expanded. But there was a shortage of labour. Britain looked for workers from Europe and the countries of the Commonwealth – the West Indies, India and Pakistan.

India achieved independence in 1947, but this did not bring instant improvement. British rule had left India an under-developed country. What had been British India was divided into two countries – India and Pakistan. This led to people being uprooted. Millions of people crossed the new borders and many were made homeless. These developments pushed young men to leave India and come to Britain to take advantage of the British economic boom. Some were professionals, others were skilled workers. But the majority were from rural backgrounds. Few hoped to stay permanently.

A woman working in a silk factory in Bradford, Yorkshire. Many Asians found work in the textile mills of Bradford, which now has a large and thriving Asian community.

One man said:

> 'My father had come here
> in 1956, one of the first
> Pakistanis to come. He
> came to improve his
> standard of living, to earn
> some money and go
> back home.'[10]

A British Asian family from Kenya arrives at Luton airport in February 1968, just before the law barred the automatic right of entry to Asians with British passports.

But many stayed on, and their families joined them. Political developments in Britain, like citizenship laws in the 1960s, also increased immigration from the Indian sub-continent and the Caribbean as people rushed to beat the new immigration ban. A Sikh ex-army officer describes how he discovered that the British government was giving work permits to those who had fought in the war. Despite having his own tailoring business in India, he came to Britain in 1964.

In the 1960s and '70s, political changes in East Africa brought educated Asians to Britain from Kenya and Uganda. Asians had settled in Africa during British rule. In 1967 Kenyan Asians with British passports were forced to leave Kenya because they were no longer wanted. In 1972 Asians were expelled from Uganda. They had to leave within ninety days and, this time, against much opposition, those with British passports were admitted to Britain as refugees.

Finding jobs

In the post-war period, jobs were plentiful in Britain. Asian doctors found employment in the newly-established NHS. Others worked on the buses and railways. Many more obtained jobs in textile mills, foundries and factories, which required a supply of cheap low-skilled labour, especially for night shifts. This explains why large Asian communities developed in places like Bradford, Leicester, Wolverhampton, Coventry and London. Here, their much-needed labour helped to rebuild industries and keep services going.

A bustling Asian shop in Bradford, Yorkshire.

Asians did not always choose to work in factories, as one first-generation settler explained:

> 'My friend's younger brother, he was very open. He said "Don't wait for any posh jobs, all Indians and Pakistanis they work in factories here. So you've got to work in factory, you've got to accept this fact. Don't wait for any special jobs. If somebody's telling you that because you are a solicitor, and you have degrees and all that, you'll get any special jobs, well, forget about it." '[11]

Asians not only had to take low-paid jobs and work unsocial hours, they also had to compromise their culture. Bhajan Singh Chadha, a Sikh accountant from Kenya, could not get a clerical job so, in the end:

> '... after a great struggle with my feelings I took off my turban, shaved my hair and applied for a job as a postman. It was not what I wanted to do, but I had come and it would have been very difficult to give up...'[12]

42

Abdul Rahman

To improve their standard of living and escape factory work, many Asians became self-employed. One such person was Abdul Rahman, who came to Britain in 1961 from Pakistan, where he owned a clothing business. In Britain, he first worked at Walls sausage factory. Then he joined Sunblest bakery, working as a dough maker for five years. In 1966 Rahman became a maintenance worker with British Airways. In 1968 he opened his own retail food business but he carried on with his airport job at night. His wife, brother and sister-in-law helped to run the business, but Rahman often worked for eighteen or twenty hours a day, seven days a week.

Marchers call for a stop to racist violence, following the death of an Asian youth, stabbed in London in June 1976.

Discrimination

At work, in housing and in education Asians faced discrimination. Racism and racial harassment were also threats. Asians organized many campaigns for equality and social justice. Vishnu Sharma and Jayaben Desai were two, among many campaigners, who became well known in the 1960s and '70s.

Vishnu Sharma came to Britain in 1957 and worked in a factory in Southall, west London before becoming a bus conductor. He led demonstrations and organized sit-ins against the National Front, a racist political party, and against discrimination in education. He was one of the founder members of the Campaign Against Racial Discrimination. Sharma also became secretary of the Indian Workers' Association. He died in 1992, aged seventy.

Jayaben Desai

Jayaben Desai was born in Gujarat, in western India, but she lived in Tanzania where her husband managed a tyre company. In 1969 they came to Britain and Jayaben, like many other Asian women, looked for employment to help the family finances. She started work at Grunwick Processing Laboratories in north-west London. Here, in 1976, she led a strike by the mainly Asian labour force against low pay, long hours, the discriminatory treatment of Asian women and for the right to join a trade union. The strikers received support from Brent Trades Council. There were mass pickets and the dispute lasted a year, attracting a great deal of publicity. The strike did not succeed, but the problems of industrial and race relations had been brought to people's attention.

Grunwick protesters with Jayaben Desai.

Asians today

Today, there are Asian businesses all over Britain, ranging from small family-run corner shops to supermarkets, hotels and garment manufacturers. Indian restaurants and Asian food have changed Britain's eating habits. These enterprises have created jobs and helped the economy. Asians are now working in all walks of life. Some have become famous in public life for their role in the arts, politics, sport and entertainment.

Kamlesh Bahl, formerly the chairperson of the Equal Opportunities Commission was awarded a CBE for services to equal opportunities.

However, like British society as a whole, the Asian community is made up of different classes of people. There are Asian millionaires, but many are poor. Some Asians are highly educated, others are not. The majority remain working class.

In 1991 there were 1,476,000 Asians in Britain, more than a third of whom were born in Britain. By 2001 the number had risen to 2,331,423. This rise is partly explained by adding the children of mixed Asian and white parentage. While proud to be Asian, they are also British, creating their own new culture. This is reflected, for instance, in Bhangra music, which combines traditional Indian music with Western dance music.

When people migrate from one country to another they carry with them their culture, labour, enterprise and capital. They are influenced by the society in which they settle and, in turn, they enrich their new country. Look around and you will see the very many ways in which Britain has benefitted from all the people, including Asians, who, over the centuries, have come to Britain.

▲ *The leader of the Bhangra band, Apache Indian, which has become popular with both Asians and non-Asian people.*

▼ *Children at a* Mela *(an Asian Carnival) in Bradford. These events are held all over Britain and are enjoyed by the whole community.*

Glossary

administration Government.

aristocracy Nobility or a class of privileged people.

ballads Songs.

capitalism An economic system based on personal wealth and profit-making.

colonialism Policy of occupying and controlling another country or part of another country.

discrimination Unfair treatment for reasons such as sex, race, nationality, ethnic origin or religion.

dynasty A succession of rulers or leaders from the same family.

exploit To use for profit.

guinea Twenty-one shillings (or £1.05).

hawker A street seller.

independence Freedom to rule one's own country.

nabob From *nawab*, an Indian word meaning nobleman or prince.

Nationalism Patriotism, or loyalty to one's own country.

plantation A large farm or estate, usually for growing one main crop.

posthumously After death.

racism To believe that some 'races' are superior to others because of physical differences, such as skin colour.

refugee A person who takes refuge in another country because of reasons such as war, persecution, race, religion or nationality.

repatriation To be sent back to one's country of origin.

repression To keep down or put down by force.

sedition An offence against the state.

shilling Twenty shillings in old money was worth £1 or 100 pennies.

stoker A fireman on a ship or steam train, who stokes a furnace with coal.

suffragette A woman who campaigned for the right to vote in elections.

under-developed country A country with resources that are not used, which has a poor economy.

valet personal servant.

Finding out more

Across Seven Seas and Thirteen Rivers: Life Stories of Pioneer Sylhetti Sailors in Britain edited by Caroline Adams (THAP Books, 1987)

Asians in Britain: 400 Years of History by Rozina Visram (Pluto Press, 2002)

Ayahs, Lascars and Princes: Indians in Britain 1700–1947 by Rozina Visram (Pluto Press, 1986)

Here to Stay: Bradford South Asian Communities (Bradford Heritage Recording Unit, 1994)

Indian Presence in Liverpool by Ashok Burman (National Museums and Galleries on the Merseyside, 2002)

Indian Voices of the Great War Selected and Introduced by David Omissi (Macmillan Press Ltd.,1999)

Reimaging Britain: 500 Years of Black and Asian History by Ron Ramdin (Pluto Press, 1999)

Roots of the Future: Ethnic Diversity in the Making of Britain by Mayerlene Frow (Commission for Racial Equality, 1996)

'South Asians in London's History' by Rozina Visram in *The Peopling of London: Fifteen Thousand Years of Settlement from Overseas*, edited by Nick Merriman (Museum of London, 1993). This book also contains a useful chapter on researching community histories and details of what is available in archives and museums.

The Other Eastenders: Kamal Chunchie and West Ham's Early Black Community by Geoffrey Bell (Eastside Community Heritage Publication, 2002)

Useful Websites

www.bl.uk/collections/britasian/britasia.html
The Asians in Britain. Oriental and India Office Collections, at the British Library. A variety of sources relating to Asians from the Indian Subcontinent.

www.movinghere.org.uk
Moving Here is the biggest database of digitised photographs, maps, objects, documents and audio items from 30 local and national archives, museums and libraries which record migration experiences of the last 200 years.

www.casbah.ac.uk
The Casbah Project includes national research resources for the history of Black and Asian people in Britain.

www.museumoflondon.org.uk
London's Voices is the museum's rich oral history collection. It explores, reflects and celebrates London's diversity through the voices, memories and opinions of Londoners.

Research

Why not help advance our knowledge and understanding of the history of Asian communities in Britain by conducting your own research? You can start in the local archives of your own area. Libraries and museums could provide you with useful information on Asian history which might help you to start your own historical research. You could also record the oral histories of older generations of friends, relatives and neighbours.

Useful addresses

Bedfordshire and Luton Archives and Record Office, County Hall, Cauldwell Street, Bedford MK42 9AP. Telephone 01234 228833
http://www.bedfordshire.gov.uk
or
http://www.casbah.ac.uk/surveys/archivereportBLARS.stm#blarscontact

Bradford Heritage Recording Unit, Bradford Industrial Muuseum, Moorside Road, Eccleshill, Bradford BD2 3HP. Tel: 01274 631756
The Bradford Heritage Recording Unit uses oral history and photography to capture the memories, reflections, contemporary attitudes and images of Bradford people of all ages, classes and races.

West Newcastle Local Studies, Benwell Library, Atkinson Road, Benwell, Newcastle Upon Tyne.

Oldham Local Studies Library, 84 Union Street, Oldham OL1 1DN. Tel 0161 911 4654
www.oldham.gov.uk/community/local_studies/

Index

Numbers in **bold** indicate subjects that are shown in pictures as well as in the text.